written by Kathy Downs
illustrated by Lorraine Arthur

I see a strange shape.
It looks as tall as a room.
Am I seeing a huge monster?
It looks like it has crooked arms.
Are they stretched out to grab me?
I start to run away and hide,
   but then I remember—

Library of Congress Catalog Card No. 81-51000

ISBN: 0-87239-475-1

I'M NOT AFRAID OF THE DARK SHADOWS!
I have a special Friend who is always with me.
Quickly I remember that this strange looking
   monster is really the funny shadow of a
   lamp.
It's the lamp that stands next to my dad's
   favorite reading chair.
I have a great idea!
I'll turn on the lamp's light to make more
   funny and strange looking shapes on the
   wall.

Once my ears were very sore. I was sick a lot.
The doctor said I had to go to the hospital.
At the hospital a nurse will give me some
    medicine to make me go to sleep.
While I'm asleep the doctor will put special
    tubes in my ears.
At first I didn't want to go to the hospital,
    but—

I'M NOT AFRAID OF GOING TO A HOSPITAL!
At the hospital there were many friendly
    people.
They all knew my name.
One man called me "Peanut."
My special Friend was with me, too.
I'm glad I went to the hospital.
My ears are not so sore now.

Last Saturday I went to a birthday party with
   my big sister.
Mother took us to the party.
When she left, she gave me a pat on the head.
She said, "You'll have a good time."
I turned around to join my sister, but where
   was she?
I couldn't find my sister.
No one I knew was at the party.
I wanted to go home, but then I remembered—

I'M NOT AFRAID TO MAKE NEW FRIENDS!
I am never alone when my special Friend is
   with me.
Soon I was playing games and had discovered
   many new friends.
Mother was right! I did have a good time!
I'm glad my special Friend was with me at the
   birthday party.

Sometimes when I'm in bed asleep, I'm suddenly awakened by the loud noise of a siren.
It is going right past our house.
The siren gets so loud I think it is right here in my room.
I want to hide under my blanket, but—

I'M NOT AFRAID OF THE LOUD SIRENS
IN THE NIGHT!

My dad says when you hear a siren it means
   someone needs help.

Maybe someone is sick or hurt.

An ambulance is taking someone quickly to a
   hospital.

Or maybe a house is on fire.

The fire truck is racing to help put out the fire.

When I hear a siren, I ask my special Friend to
   take care of the people who need help.

My Bible school is having a special program.
My teacher wants me to say a poem for the
 program.
There will be many people at the program.
What if I forget what to say?
Then I remember—

I'M NOT AFRAID TO SAY A POEM IN FRONT OF MANY PEOPLE.

My special Friend has promised to help me in everything I do.

With His help I know I can say the poem in front of all those people.

AND I DID!

My teacher said he was proud of me.

Aunt Molly invited us over to her house for
    dinner.
She had fixed a special food.
I didn't like the way it looked.
I didn't like the way it smelled.
I was sure I wouldn't like the taste, but then I
    remembered—

I'M NOT AFRAID TO TRY NEW FOODS!

At our house we play a game when my mother cooks a new food.

I have to take six bites because I'm six years old.

I always win! When I have eaten the six bites, I have found another new food that I like.

It didn't take long to clean up my plate at Aunt Molly's.

Of course, I thank my special Friend for the good food my Aunt Molly cooked for me.

Today is the first day of school.
My mother keeps telling me to hurry!
"Hurry and get dressed!"
"Hurry and comb your hair!"
"Hurry and eat your breakfast!"
"Hurry and brush your teeth!"
Hurry! Hurry! Hurry!
I don't feel like hurrying.
I keep thinking about my new teacher.
I wonder if she will like me.
Will she be friendly?
Will she be grouchy?
Suddenly I remember—

I'M NOT AFRAID OF NEW TEACHERS!
My special Friend is with me when I go to school.
Before my mother has to tell me one more time
    to "hurry," I quickly grab my school bag and
    dash out the door.
I want to be the first one to meet my new teacher.
My teacher is probably anxious to meet me, too!

Some people are superstitious.
That means they are afraid to do something they think will cause them to have "bad luck."

I'M NOT AFRAID—
of having bad luck because I walk under a ladder.

of having seven years of bad luck when I have broken a mirror.

of having bad luck when I wear the number 13.

of taking a test at school without a rabbit's foot for "good luck."

I'M NOT AFRAID.
My special Friend always helps me to do my very best.

I'M NOT AFRAID—
   of the dark shadows.
   of going to a hospital.
   of loud sirens in the night.
   to say a poem in front of many people.
   to try new foods.
   of new teachers.
   of causing myself to have bad luck.
We are not afraid because our special Friend is
   Jesus.

Jesus is with us wherever we go.
Jesus helps us do our best.